Index

Historic sites

Imperial Castle	Page 5
Albrecht Duerer's House	Page 6
Schuerstab House	Page 8
St. Sebald Church	Page 10
Town Hall	Page 12
Beautiful Fountain	Page 14
Church of Our Lady	Page 16
Hospital of the Holy Spirit	Page 18
St. Lawrence Church	Page 20
The Way of Human Rights	Page 22
Opera	Page 24
Courtroom 600	Page 26
Documentation Centre Nazi Party Rally Grounds	Page 28
Christmas Market	Page 30
Nuremberg gingerbread	Page 32
Nuremberg Bratwurst	Page 34
Vegetables from the Knoblauchsland	Page 36
Imprint	Page 38

Kaiserburg

Die Burg, erbaut ab 1140, ist das Wahrzeichen der Stadt Nürnberg. Sie besteht aus der Kaiserburg, der Burggrafenburg sowie den reichsstädtischen Bauten. Auf der Kaiserburg hielten sich im Mittelalter alle Kaiser und Könige des Heiligen Römischen Reiches auf. Besichtigt werden können der Palas mit Doppelkapelle, das Kaiserburg-Museum, der Tiefe Brunnen sowie der Sinwellturm. Von der Freiung aus hat man einen wunderbaren Blick über die Altstadt.

Imperial Castle

The castle, built in 1140, is the number one landmark of Nuremberg. It is composed of the Imperial Castle, the Castle of the Count ("Burggrafenburg"), as well as the imperial city buildings. All emperors and kings of the Holy Roman Empire stayed at the Imperial Castle in the Middle Ages. The Palas, with the double-chapel, the Imperial Castle Museum, the Deep Well and the Sinwell Tower are all open for visitors. The castle courtyard gives a panoramic view over the roofs of Nuremberg.

Albrecht-Dürer-Haus

Der deutsche Maler, Zeichner und Kupferstecher Albrecht Dürer (1471–1528) zählt zu den bedeutendsten und vielseitigsten Persönlichkeiten der Kunstgeschichte. Zu seinen bekanntesten Werken zählen sein Selbstbildnis und der „Dürer-Hase". Zwanzig Jahre lang wohnte der Maler in diesem mächtigen Fachwerkhaus. Es ist in Nordeuropa das einzige Künstlerhaus aus dem 16. Jahrhundert, das noch erhalten ist. Heute ist das Haus ein Museum.

Albrecht Duerer's House

The german painter, drawer and copper engraver, Albrecht Duerer (1471–1528) is one of the most important and versatile personalities of art history. Among his famous works are his self-portrait and his painting of the "Young Hare" ("Duerer Hase"). The artist lived in a big timbered house for 20 years. It is the only preserved artists' house from the 16th century in northern Europe. Nowadays the house is a museum.

Schürstabhaus

Das Haus zeigt einen Querschnitt von fast 750 Jahren Nürnberger Architekturgeschichte – vom Mittelalter bis zur Neuzeit. Hier wohnte die Patrizierfamilie Schürstab, deren Familienmitglieder jahrhundertelang im Nürnberger Rat vertreten waren.

Schuerstab House

The house is a cross-section of the history of Nuremberg's architecture. Starting from the Middle Ages to the modern age. This was the residence of the patrician family Schuerstab, whose family members where represented in the council of Nuremberg.

Sebalduskirche

Die Sebalduskirche ist die ältere der beiden großen Stadtpfarrkirchen Nürnbergs. Sie wurde um 1215 als dreischiffige spätromanische Pfeilerbasilika mit zwei Chören erbaut. Bereits 1309 wurden die ursprünglichen Seitenschiffe erweitert und im gotischen Stil verändert. Das bedeutendste Kunstwerk der Kirche ist das Sebaldusgrab, das auf vier Delfinen und zwölf Schnecken ruht. Hier sind die Reliquien des katholischen St. Sebald aufbewahrt, was in einer evangelisch-lutherischen Kirche eine Besonderheit ist.

St. Sebald Church

St. Sebald Church is the oldest of the biggest two parish churches in Nuremberg. It was built in 1215 as a three-nave late Romanesque Gothic pillar basilica with two chancels. Already in 1309, the original side aisles were broadened and changed to Gothic style. The most important artwork in this church is the grave of Sebaldus, which is standing on four dolphins and twelve snails. Here lie the relics of the catholic St. Sebald, which is unusual for an Evangelical Lutheran church.

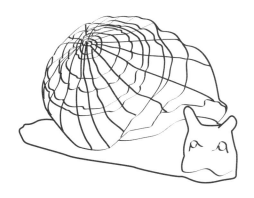

Altes Rathaus

Alle vom 14. bis 17. Jahrhundert entstandenen Bauten des Nürnberger Rathauses nennt man „Altes Rathaus". Am repräsentativsten ist der sogenannte Wolff'sche Bau. Er ist im Stil eines italienischen Palastes errichtet. Seine etwa 80 Meter lange Schaufassade ist streng gegliedert und geprägt von drei prunkvollen Portalen, auf deren Giebeln das große und kleine Stadtwappen sowie das Reichswappen dargestellt sind.

Town Hall

All buildings of Nuremberg's city hall, built between 14th and 17th century are called "Town Hall". The so-called "Wolff'sche Bau" is the most representative building. Its style of the construction was inspired by Italian palaces. The 80 meters (262 ft) facade is strictly divided and has three splendid portals, which have coats of arms on their gables, i.e. the big and smaller municipal coat, as well as the imperial coat of arms.

Schöner Brunnen

Der Schöne Brunnen mit seinem 19 Meter hohen Aufbau steht auf dem Hauptmarkt. In seiner heutigen Form wurde er um 1390 erbaut. Auf vier Etagen verteilt, stellen vierzig farbig bemalte Figuren das damalige Weltbild anschaulich dar. Im Brunnengitter befindet sich ein goldener Ring. Eine Legende besagt, dass wer daran dreht, drei Wünsche erfüllt bekommt.

Beautiful Fountain

The Beautiful Fountain is 19 meters (62 ft) high and stands on the main market in the old town of Nuremberg. Its current form was built around 1390. Forty colored figures are arranged on four levels around the fountain, which represented the world view at that time. A legend says that if you turn the golden ring embedded in the fence around the fountain you will have three wishes granted.

Frauenkirche

1355 wurde die Frauenkirche im Auftrag Karls IV. auf den Grund-mauern der bei einem Judenpogrom zerstörten Synagoge erbaut. Im Auftrag der Stadt ließ Adam Kraft von 1506–1509 den westli-chen Giebel der Kirche umgestalten. Dabei wurde zur Erinnerung an Kaiser Karl IV. eine Kunstuhr eingebaut, die bis heute täglich um 12.00 Uhr die Huldigung der sieben Kurfürsten an den Kaiser, das sogenannte Männleinlaufen, zeigt.

Church of Our Lady

In 1355 the Church of Our Lady was built on behalf of Charles IV. on the foundation walls of a synagogue, which was destroyed earlier during a Jewish pogrom. Adam Kraft had the western gable of the church redesigned between 1506–1509 by order of the city. An art clock was built in, in remembrance of the emperor Charles IV. Every day at 12 am the clock shows the tribute of the seven Electors, the so called "Maennleinlaufen".

Heilig-Geist-Spital

Der reiche Nürnberger Bürger Konrad Groß gründete 1339 – zu seinem Seelenheil – das Heilig-Geist-Spital. Einerseits war es ein Krankenhaus, andererseits ein Altersheim für mittellose arbeitsunfähige ältere Menschen. Reiche Bürger mussten Wohn- und Kostgeld zahlen. Da die Einrichtung im 15. Jahrhundert erweitert wurde, erfolgte die Überbauung der Pegnitz mit den zwei brückenartigen Gebäuden.

Hospital of the Holy Spirit

In 1339 Konrad Gross, a rich Nuremberger founded the Hospital of the Holy Spirit to seek the salvation of his soul. It was used as a hospital and as a home for old people, who were penniless or unfit for work. Wealthy citizens had to pay housing benefit and board wages. During the expansion of the establishment in the 15th century, two bridge-like buildings were constructed over the river Pegnitz.

St. Lorenz

Der Baubeginn der Lorenzkirche liegt um 1250. Ursprünglich wurde sie als dreischiffige hochgotische Basilika errichtet und im 15. Jahrhundert um den gewaltigen spätgotischen Hallenchor erweitert. Die 77 Meter hohen Doppeltürme sowie die beeindruckende Westfassade mit dem figurenreichen Portal und der Rosette entstanden Mitte des 14. Jahrhunderts. Die zwei bedeutendsten Kunstwerke sind der Englische Gruß von Veit Stoß und das Sakramentshaus von Adam Kraft.

St. Lawrence Church

The construction of the St. Lawrence Church started around 1250. It was originally erected as a three nave, high Gothic basilica and only in the 15th century the big hall choir in late Gothic style was added. The 77 meters (253 ft) high twin towers as well as the impressive west front with the figure-rich portal and the rose window were built in the middle of the 14th century. The two most important works of art are the Angelic Salutation ("Englischer Gruss") by Veit Stoss and the tabernacle ("Sakramentshaus") by Adam Kraft.

Straße der Menschenrechte

Nürnberg ist die „Stadt des Friedens und der Menschenrechte". Sichtbares Zeichen dafür ist die „Straße der Menschenrechte". Mit diesem begehbaren Kunstwerk beim Germanischen Nationalmuseum hat der israelische Künstler Dani Karavan ein einzigartiges Kunstwerk geschaffen. 27 acht Meter hohe Betonsäulen bilden einen stilisierten Triumphbogen. In jeder Säule ist ein Artikel der „Allgemeinen Erklärung der Menschenrechte" in deutscher sowie in jeweils einer anderen Sprache eingemeißelt.

The Way of Human Rights

Nuremberg is "the city of peace and human rights". A visible sign is the "Way of Human Rights". This passable art work next to the Germanic National Museum is a unique piece by the Jewish artist Dani Karavan. The 27 eight meters (26 ft) high concrete pillars form a stylized triumphal arch. Each pillar has an article of the "Universal Declaration of Human Rights", carved in German and in one other, foreign language.

23

Opernhaus

Bereits 1905 zogen Oper und Operette an dieses „Neue Stadt-
theater am Ring". Die Innenausstattung dieses ehemals schönsten
Jugendstil-Theaters in Deutschland gefiel Hitler nicht. Er ließ die
Einrichtung 1935 entfernen und in vereinfachtem Neubarock umge-
stalten. Beachtenswert sind unter anderem die überlebensgroßen
Figuren auf dem Giebel des Haupteinganges, die den Lustigen
Rat, die Noris und den Meistersinger darstellen.

Opera

The opera and operetta moved to the "New municipal theater at
the beltway" ("Neues Stadttheater am Ring"). Hitler did not like
the interior decoration of the former most beautiful Art Nouveau
theater of Germany. He had the furnishing removed and redesigned into simplified neo-baroque in 1935. The larger-than-life
statues on top of the gable over the main entrance show the court
jester, "Noris" and the master singer ("Meistersinger").

Saal 600

Im Schwurgerichtssaal des Nürnberger Justizpalastes wurden die Prozesse gegen die Hauptverantwortlichen des NS-Regimes geführt. 21 Angeklagte mussten sich hier wegen Kriegsverbrechen sowie wegen Verbrechen gegen Frieden und Menschlichkeit verantworten. Im Dachgeschoss des Gerichtsgebäudes befindet sich die Informations- und Dokumentationsstätte „Memorium Nürnberger Prozesse".

Courtroom 600

The trials of the main culprits of the Nazi regime were carried out in the courtroom of the Palace of Justice in Nuremberg. 21 accused had to stand trial for war crimes and crime against freedom and humanity. Now there is an information and documentation center in the attic of the courthouse.

Dokumentationszentrum Reichsparteitagsgelände

Das Dokuzentrum ist ein Museum und befindet sich in der von den Nationalsozialisten konzipierten, unvollendet gebliebenen Kongresshalle des ehemaligen Reichsparteitagsgeländes. Verschiedene Dauerausstellungen beschäftigen sich mit den Ursachen, Zusammenhängen und Folgen der nationalsozialistischen Gewaltherrschaft.

Documentation Centre Nazi Party Rally Grounds

The Documentation Centre is a museum located in the unfinished conference hall of the Nazi party rally grounds. Various permanent displays take a close look on the reasons, connections and consequences of the Nazi dictatorship.

Christkindlesmarkt

Nürnberg ist in der ganzen Welt als „die Weihnachtsstadt" bekannt. Der Hauptmarkt mit den während des Christkindlesmarktes rund 180 geschmückten Buden und der Frauenkirche im Hintergrund ist immer einen Besuch wert. Eröffnet wird der Markt durch das Nürnberger Christkind, das alle zwei Jahre neu gewählt wird.

Christmas Market

Nuremberg is known in the world to be the city of christmas. The main market square with the decorated stands and the Church of Our Lady in the background is always worth a visit. The market is opened by the Nuremberg "Christkind", who is elected every two years.

Nürnberger Lebkuchen

Lebkuchen aus Nürnberg gehen in die ganze Welt. Und die Tradition der Lebkuchenproduktion reicht bis ins Mittelalter zurück. Grundlage für die Lebkuchenherstellung war der Wildhonig aus den Reichswäldern. Die exotischen Gewürze brachten die Nürnberger Kaufleute über Venedig oder Antwerpen in die Stadt.

Nuremberg gingerbread

Gingerbread from Nuremberg is known around the world. The tradition of gingerbread production dates to medieval times. Back then it was made of wild honey from the imperial forest grounds. The exotic herbs were brought to town by the Nuremberg tradesmen following the route through Venice or Antwerp.

Nürnberger Bratwurst

Die Rezeptur der Nürnberger Bratwurst wurde bereits im Jahre 1313 vom Rat der Reichsstadt Nürnberg erstmals festgelegt und war von Anfang an auf beste Qualität des Ausgangsmaterials ausgerichtet. Die Nürnberger Bratwurst wiegt rund 25 g und ist so klein, dass man früher sagte, sie müsse durch ein Schlüsselloch passen.

Nuremberg Bratwurst

The recipe of the Nuremberg sausages was set by the council of the imperial city Nuremberg for the first time in 1313, which layed utmost emphasis on the quality of the main ingredients. The Nuremberg Bratwurst weighs around 25 g (0.9 oz) and is small enough that in the past people said it should fit through a keyhole.

35

Gemüse aus dem Knoblauchsland

Das Knoblauchsland ist ein Gemüseanbaugebiet am Stadtrand von Nürnberg und gilt als eines der größten zusammenhängenden Anbaugebiete seiner Art in Deutschland. Erschlossen wurde es bereits im 8. Jahrhundert und wie der Name schon sagt, wurden vor allem Knoblauch und Zwiebeln angebaut. Heute gibt es ein breit gefächertes Angebot, das u. a. auf dem Hauptmarkt verkauft wird.

Vegetables from the Knoblauchsland

The "Knoblauchsland" is an area of vegetable cultivation on the outskirts of Nuremberg. It is known as the biggest cultivation area of this kind in Germany. It has been made accessible in the 8th century, where mostly garlic and onions were grown. That's where the name of the area originates from. Garlic translates into "Knoblauch" in German. Today there is a wide selection, which can be bought on the main market square amongst others.

Impressum

Imprint

NÜRNBERG
kennenlernen & ausmalen
discover & color

Herausgeber/Publisher
context verlag Nürnberg
www.context-mv.de

ISBN 978-3-939645-99-3
1. Auflage/Edition,
November 2016

Copyright © 2016
Alle Rechte vorbehalten./
All rights reserved.

**Konzeption und Text/
Conception and text**
Petra Kluger

Lektorat/Editorial office
Sandra Riedmüller

Übersetzung/Translation
Lisa Giesinger

**Grafik/Graphic design, Illustration,
Produktion/Production**
Winkler Werbung Werbeagentur GmbH
www.winkler-werbung.de

Bibliografische Information der Deutschen Nationalbibliothek: Die Deutsche
Nationalbibliothek verzeichnet diese
Publikation in der Deutschen National-
bibliografie, detaillierte bibliografische
Daten sind im Internet über
http://dnb.d-nb.de abrufbar.